P9-DMT-285

_____

PRESENTED TO

_____

FROM

_____

DATE

LOVING WORDS
Every Woman Wants to Hear

Rekindling

Love

and

Intimacy

ED ANDERSON
AND
JOHN E. PETERSON

COUNTRYMAN

LOVE

Love, a state of mind

Text copyright © 1998 by John E. Peterson and Edwin P. Anderson

Published by J. Countryman®
a division of Thomas Nelson, Inc., Nashville, Tennessee 37214

All Scripture references are from the New King James Version (NKJV),
© copyright 1979, 1980, 1982 by Thomas Nelson, Inc.,
and are used by permission.

A J. Countryman book.

Editorial development and design production by
Koechel Peterson & Associates, Minneapolis, MN.

Photography by Tom Henry

ISBN: 08499-5402-9

Printed and bound in Belgium

only the wise or lucky ever find.

And having found it,

only the brave

can make it flourish

until the grave.

INTRODUCTION

Women like romance. And let's not forget that men enjoy it, too. Though no one has a foolproof formula for romance, words can make the difference. Romantic Loving Words can be fun, playful, serious, or silly. They can be healing, encouraging, satisfying, and wonderful. Sometimes they come at us all at once, but often just a little at a time.

No matter how romantic words are used, you are a lucky person if you are in a relationship where Loving Words are shared like this love note

These are my thoughts of you

TO MY WIFE

Remember how hard it used to be for us to say,
"Good-bye," even when it was for just a few hours?
That's what I felt today as you left. I didn't want you to go.
I wished I could change today into a weekend so we could
get away and be together. I just had to leave a phone message
for you at work to let you know I was thinking of you.
I wanted you to know how I looked forward to you getting home,
to hold you again, and to hear you say those words of love
that I love so much. It may sound a bit corny to say,
but I am the luckiest man alive to have you as my wife.
God sure knew what He was doing when
He brought you into my life.

Your Husband

Cliff

See how Loving Words can make a difference? When Loving Words are expressed, the true feelings each feels for the other become clearer, and very little compares to it. If you've never tried expressing your feelings to your mate, then you are in for some wonderful romantic surprises.

LOVING

"I CAN'T WAIT TO SEE YOU."

love

"*If I had to*

do it all over

"*No matter how hard I try or*

how many words I use, I could

never adequately express what

you mean to me."

again, I'd do

it with you."

"The best part of the day is when

"*I can't really know you*

"*We can only learn*

to love by loving."

IRIS MURDOCH

with my eyes

and ears; only my heart can."

"The best part
"TENDER MOMENTS ARE SPENT WITH YOU."
of the day is when

I come home

to you."

"Nothing
compares
with the time
we are
together."

ome home to you."

"I can't wait to see you."

"Live joyfully with your wife."

ECCLESIASTES 9:9

ROMANCE

There are two types of romance,
obligatory and *spontaneous.*

Both are important. All men are advised not to overlook
the obligatory, but, make no mistake about it, spontaneous
romance is more genuinely romantic.

Here's the difference. **Obligatory** romance includes
the things you are obligated to do, such as celebrating
your wife's birthday, getting her a Christmas gift,
remembering your anniversary, sending valentines on
Valentine's Day, remembering Mother's Day. **Spontaneous**
romance includes all of the above if you do it in a unique
and totally unexpected way and any unplanned gesture
of love—such as flowers for no special reason. Little
surprises, big surprises. Surprise dates in the middle of
the week or in the middle of the night. Champagne
toasts, candlelight dinners, weekend getaways, massages,
love letters, romantic movies. Moonlight walks.

"The best portion of a good man's life are his little, nameless, unremembered acts of kindness and of love."

WILLIAM
WORDSWORTH

HOW DO I LOVE THEE?

How do I love thee? Let me count the ways.

I love thee to the depth and breadth and height

My soul can reach, when feeling out of sight

For the ends of Being and ideal Grace.

I love thee to the level of every day's

Most quiet need, by sun and candle-light.

I love thee freely, as men strive for Right;

I love thee purely, as they turn from Praise.

I love thee with the passion put to use

In my old griefs, and with my childhood's faith.

I love thee with a love I seemed to lose

With my lost saints,—I love thee with the breath,

Smiles, tears, of all my life!—and, if God choose,

I shall but love thee better after death.

Elizabeth Barrett Browning

"Turn your

eyes away

from me,

for they

have

overcome

me."

SONG OF
SOLOMON 6:5

"I treasure the look you give me when you think I'm not looking."

Have you ever caught your

wife looking at you with love?

You turn around and her eyes

are on you, and all of a sudden

there's a shower of warmth. It's

a marvelous thing to feel.

> "If instead of a gem, or even a flower,
>
> we should cast the gift of a loving
>
> thought into the heart of a friend, that
>
> would be giving as the angels give."
>
> **GEORGE MACDONALD**

"*My love,*

my perfect one . . ."

SONG OF SOLOMON 6:9

"I thought it was impossible to love someone as much as I love you— until I met you."

Nothing on earth comes close to

finding the love of your life and making

it a love that lasts a lifetime.

"If God were to grant me just one wish, I'd wish this day and this moment would last forever."

Regardless of what the statisticians tell us, true love can and does last forever. If that weren't true, then what's "forever" for?

Frances Goldwyn was once asked what it was like to be married to the same man for more than thirty-five years. "It gets worse every day," Mrs. Goldwyn responded. "Thirty-five years ago I told Sam to come home and I'd fix him lunch. He's been coming home for lunch every day for thirty-five years."

"So Jacob served seven years for Rachel, and they seemed only a few days to him because of the love he had for her."

GENESIS 29:20

"Keep your heart

with all diligence,

for out of it spring

the issues of life."

PROVERBS 4:23

"You Are the Love of My life"

My love is yours to throw away,

Or keep for yet another day,

And with it all I am I give

For one brief moment of your love

That bids me live

And strive with all my soul to earn

What love you spare me in return.

For he who takes but never gives

May last for years

But never lives.

Kent Collier

"Shall I compare thee to a summer's day?
Thou art more lovely and more temperate:
Rough winds do shake the darling buds of May,
And summer's lease has all too short a date:
Sometimes too hot the eye of heaven shines,
And often is his gold complexion dimmed;
And every fair from fair sometimes declines,
By chance, or nature's changing course untrimm'd;
But thy eternal summer shall not fade,
Nor lose possession of that fair thou ow'st
Nor shall death brag thou wander'st in his shade,
When in eternal lines of time thou grow'st;
So long as men can breathe, or eyes can see,
So long lives this, and gives life to thee."

William Shakespeare

"When I gave my heart away

t was to you, forever."

kindness

"I have a surprise for you."

"*The aroma*

from your

kitchen sends

loving

messages."

"MY HEAR

"That was a great meal."

"You rest.

I'll take

care of that."

"Think twice before
you speak, especially
if you intend to say
what you think."

UNKNOWN

"That was a nice thing

ELLS ME YOU'LL BE THERE FOR ME."

you did for me.

Thank you."

Surprise her.
Let her know you've

Her last words to you as you said "Good-bye," you can't get them out of your mind. She has that way of teasing you with her eyes. She knows it, and you love it. Your mind focuses forward to later on today when you'll see her again, and in your arms will be a surprise you can hardly wait to give her. You can't wait to see her and let her know you've been thinking of her all day.

been thinking of her all day.

"And this I pray, that your love may

abound still more and more."

PHILIPPIANS 1:9

"Let's get c

"Love is not
thinking about it;
it is doing it.
It is loving."
ERIC BUTTERWORTH

sitter for next Friday.

I have a surprise for you."

Planning, in and of itself, does not destroy spontaneity;

it merely creates opportunity.

"*Whatever your hand finds to do,*

do it with your might."

ECCLESIASTES 9:10

There are times to work "overtime" at work,

and there are times to

WORK "OVERTIME" ON

YOUR RELATIONSHIP.

"If it's okay with you

"Love is, above all,

the gift of oneself."

JEAN ANNULI

"I am my beloved's,
and his desire is toward me."

SONG OF SOLOMON 7:10

et's just stay an extra day."

"Honey, is there anything

Instead of the Golden Rule—

do unto others as you would have them do unto you—

LIVE THE PLATINUM RULE

IN YOUR MARRIAGE:

Do unto your wife what she wants done unto her.

I can do for you?"

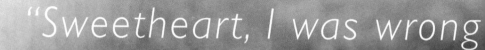

"Sweetheart, I was wrong

By being open and honest with

each other, the two of you will

be drawn together in ways you

never dreamed possible.

"Will you forgive me?"

"Life catches up with us and teaches us to love and forgive each other."

COLLINS

TAKE TIME TO NOTICE . . .
*expressing gratitude
in the now*

Take time to notice the little

things your wife does to

make your house a home.

She does it because she loves

your children. She does it

because she loves you.

"With you

our kids are

THANK

"Her children rise up

and call her blessed;

Her husband also,

and he praises her."

PROVERBS 31:28

for a mother, YOU

some of the luckiest children alive."

MAKING IT

"To be marooned on an island
with you...I can't imagine"

"How fair and pleasant you are,

O love, with your delights."

SONG OF SOLOMON 7:6

HAPPEN

anything more romantic."

"Love is the only force

on earth that can be

dispensed or received

in an extreme manner,

without any qualifications,

without any harm to

the giver or to the

receiver."

MARTIN LUTHER KING JR.

affirmation

"When you laugh,

I can't help but laugh

with you."

"Your kitchen is an oasis for me, ful

"You are so much fun."

"No one could ever take your place."

"If I had to do it

all over again,

I'd do it with you."

f love and creativity."

"You have brought so

"No man is luckier than I am."
much joy to my life."

No one could ever

take your place.

You are one-of-a-kind

and very special to me.

"If I had to do it

TOGE

You come to realize that after all these years your wife has stood by you when she didn't have to, contributed great energy to your marriage and didn't have to, and listened to your complaints and didn't have to. Why did she do what she didn't have to? Because she loves you and doesn't have to.

ll over again, I'd do it with you."

"Yours Forever"

The measure of our lives is not found in our

income, our bank balance, or status symbols.

It's found in the hugs and kisses and symbols of

undying love we share each day.

"There is only one

happiness in life, to

love and be loved."

GEORGE SAND

"I'm luckier than any man ha

"Like a lily among thorns, so is

my love among the daughters."

Song of Solomon 2:2

Don't be afraid to let everyone know how

lucky and blessed you are to have this

extraordinary woman as your wife.

right to be,

nd it's because I have you."

"A word fitly spoken is

like apples of gold

in settings of silver."

PROVERBS 25:11

Listen to your heart,

then speak from your heart.

asily get lost in there with you,
never come out,
and never care."

"Those who have the largest hearts have the soundest understanding: and he is the truest who can forget himself."

WILLIAM HAZLITT

"[Be] knit together in love."

<small>COLOSSIANS 2:2</small>

"Out of all the couples
in all the world,
I'm glad we're us."

Shared memories and

experiences weave the tapestry

of your lives into one.

"So many memories...
so many
    special moments...

What golden memories you have.

And the great part of it is, it isn't over.

so many
reasons to love you."

"Set me as a seal upon your heart,

as a seal upon your arm;

for love is as strong as death."

SONG OF SOLOMON 8:6

"What lies behind us,

and what lies before

us, are tiny matters

compared to what

lies within us."

UNKNOWN

LOVING concern

"I'll fix dinner.

Take a hot bath,

and when you're

done we'll eat."

"Is there

anything

I can do

for you?"

"I know you had

an accident.

Are you all right?"

"When you are sad, I am glad

WORDS

"ARE YOU TAKING GOOD CARE OF YOURSELF?"

"I can see you are

feeling better."

"I will always be here for you."

"These are for you."

an comfort you."

"Please tell me what you are feeling."

"You just relax.
I'll take care of it."

Relationships are about loving,

and living, and caring, and sharing,

and trying, and doing, and

learning, and being.

MAINTAINING PERSPECTIVE

There are days in everyone's life when,

due to the pressures of living, we lose perspective.

We go stale. We find ourselves wondering,

"What's the point of all this?"

When that happens, and it will, read 1 Corinthians 13.

We were created to give love and to receive love.

LIFE IS MOST MEANINGFUL
WHEN WE LIVE TO LOVE.

1 CORINTHIANS 13

"Though I speak with the tongues of men and of angels, but have not love, I have become sounding brass or a clanging cymbal. And though I have the gift of prophecy, and understand all mysteries and all knowledge, and though I have all faith, so that I could remove mountains, but have not love, I am nothing. And though I bestow all my goods to feed the poor, and though I give my body to be burned, but have not love, it profits me nothing.

Loving Words from the Bible

"Love suffers long and is kind; love does not envy; love does not parade itself, is not puffed up; does not behave rudely, does not seek its own, is not provoked, thinks no evil; does not rejoice in iniquity, but rejoices in the truth; bears all things, believes all things, hopes all things, endures all things.

"Love never fails. But whether there are prophecies, they will fail; whether there are tongues, they will cease; whether there is knowledge, it will vanish away. For we know in part and we prophesy in part. But when that which is perfect has come, then that which is in part will be done away.

"When I was a child, I spoke as a child, I understood as a child, I thought as a child; but when I became a man, I put away childish things. For now we see in a mirror, dimly, but then face to face. Now I know in part, but then I shall know just as I also am known.

"And now abide faith, hope, love, these

three; but the greatest of these is love."

—1 Corinthians 13

Romance is a state of mind.

If you have the *right* mindset you can make something as trivial as changing your wife's tire a romantic event.

"Love is that condition in which

the happiness of another person

is essential to your own."

ROBERT A. HEINLEIN

"Let no one seek his own, but each one the other's well-being."

1 Corinthians 10:23

"I've watchec

ou grow with new challenges.
I'm proud of you!"

Love stories don't have "happy" endings…

because they don't have endings.

"Being close like this...

"To everything

there is a season,

a time for every

purpose under

heaven."

1 JOHN 4:18

nothing else seems to matter."

Romance is not instinctual;

it's a learned behavior.

Anyone can learn. And best of all,

it's the most fun behavior to learn.

LOVING

respect

"YOU ARE MY HERO."

"No one

has ever

done that

for me."

"You are an

inspiration to me."

"I seem to see thin

"Your hands

are etched

with care for

others."

WORDS

"I want to take

"There is no end to your kindness."

you to dinner.

Which restaurant do you prefer?"

You've contributed

ifferently when I am with you."

a great deal

to my life."

"That which we
understand we
can't blame."
GOETHE

"Every time I look at our
children I'm reminded of

EXPRESSING
GRATITUDE
IN THE NOW

"This woman was full

of good works and

charitable deeds."

ACTS 9:36

all the joy you've given me."

"At moments like this,
    I can feel God tapping me o

he shoulder and whispering,

'This is as good as it gets.' "

"Behold, you are fair, my love!"

SONG OF SOLOMON 1:15

"Life is short and we never have enough time for gladdening the hearts of those who travel the way with us. O, be swift to love! Make haste to be kind."

UNKNOWN

E x p r e s s i o

"Your cheeks are lovely with ornaments, Your neck with chains of gold."

SONG OF SOLOMON 1:10

These are for you.

Give me that great smile of yours.

That was a great meal.

These flowers are for you.

I have a surprise for you.

That was such a nice thing you did for me.

You rest; I'll take care of that.

You've contributed a great deal to my life.

No one has ever done that for me.

Your children are loved by you.

Whenever I smell those special cookies you make,

I count myself lucky.

ns of Love

I'll fix dinner. Take a hot bath, and when you're done we'll eat.

What can I do to help?

The aroma from your kitchen sends loving messages.

Are you sure you don't need my help?

What are your favorite flowers?

People enjoy being with you.

I want to take you to dinner. Which restaurant do you prefer?

Your touch says love.

I feel good about loving you.

I love being in your life.

"Remembe

"We can only

learn to love

by loving."

IRIS MURDOCH

Take a breath. Give yourself a chance to relax

when we *fell in love?*

and once again be reminded of why the two

of you fell in love in the first place.

"Rejoice with the wife of your youth....

And always be enraptured with her love."

PROVERBS 5:18, 19

"I see the hand o

Most people believe their relationship is special, one-of-a-kind. They believe they didn't just happen to find each other but something—some power, something bigger than the both of them—put them together. No other explanation satisfies. These couples look at their relationship as meaningful and purposeful, a love designed in heaven.

God in our relationship."

"Who can find a virtuous wife?

For her worth is far above rubies.

The heart of her husband safely trusts her."

PROVERBS 31:10, 11

Few pleasures in life exceed

giving, especially when giving

the gift of yourself. When you

say "I'm yours," you have given

your wife the only thing that

really matters to her.

"Nothing gives me more joy

...han knowing I'm yours!"

"We make a living
by what we get,
we make a life by
what we give."
**WINSTON
CHURCHILL**

YOURS

RESOURCES

> "The king loved Esther.... Then the king made a great
> feast, the Feast of Esther, for all his officials and servants;
> and he proclaimed a holiday in the provinces and gave
> gifts according to the generosity of a king."
>
> ESTHER 2:17, 18

Save up for that special romantic trip. Plan for it, talk
about it, dream about it…but, do it! Need we say more?

Romantic Vacation Spots

A FEW SUGGESTIONS, SOME OBVIOUS, SOME NOT SO OBVIOUS.

San Francisco
Sanibel Island
Hawaii
Quebec City
The Caymans
Cape Cod
The Boundary Waters
Door County
Florida Keys
Durango, Colorado
Broadmoor Inn,
Colorado Springs
Banff
Bayfield, Wisconsin

The Outer Banks
Austin, Texas
St. Croix
Mackinac Island
New Orleans
Bar Harbor, Maine
The South of France
Cadillac Mountain,
Maine, at sunrise
Venice
Salzburg
Paris
Big Sur
Captiva Island

> *"The time of singing has come."*
>
> SONG OF SOLOMON 2:11

Few things set the tone better for a romantic evening than music. You want to say something with music that conveys warmth. Music can be one of your best allies. Take time to choose before snapping just any CD into the player. Arrange the CDs in order, set the stereo volume at a conversational level, and forget about them; this isn't a concert, the music's background stuff. No hard rock, please! Think "romantic."

Romantic Music/Musicians

PERFORMERS, COMPOSERS:

Phil Collins
Luther Vandross
Tony Bennett
Beethoven
Harry Connick, Jr.
The Carpenters
Jim Croce
Debussy
Pat Matheny

The Jackie Gleason Orchestra
Nat King Cole and Natale Cole
Kenny G.
Frank Sinatra
Barry White
101 Strings
Maurice Chevalier

SONGS AND ARTISTS
TO CONSIDER

"Just the Way You Are"
BY BILLY JOEL

"Fields of Gold"
BY STING

"You Are So Beautiful"
BY JOE COCKER

*"The Way You Look
Tonight"* AND
*"I Left My Heart in San
Francisco"*
BY TONY BENNETT

"Lady in Red"
BY CHRIS DEBURGH

"Dancing Cheek to Cheek"
BY FRANK SINATRA

"Perhaps Love"
BY JOHN DENVER AND
PLACIDO DOMINGO

"Out of Africa"
(SOUNDTRACK)

"Someone Like You"
BY VAN MORRISON

"A String of Pearls"
BY GLENN MILLER

"The Wings of Love"
BY DAVID MORRIS
OR BETTE MIDLER

"Against All Odds"
BY PHIL COLLINS

"Longer"
BY DAN FOGELBERG

"My Funny Valentine"
BY CHET BAKER

"As Time Goes By"
BY JIMMY DURANTE OR
DEWEY WILSON

"The Power of Love"
BY CELINE DION

"God respects me when I work, but he loves me when I sing."

UNKNOWN

IMPORTANT PHONE NUMBERS EVERY MARRIED MAN* NEEDS TO KNOW

(*And for a few who are thinking about marriage.)

Okay, guys, you may forget your e-mail address.

Your fax number. Your Social Security number.

Or even the combination to your gym locker. But,

in addition to your anniversary and your wife's

birthday, don't forget these!

We've divided them into four categories. Of course

there are many other numbers you might also want

ready access to, but these cover most of the essentials.

Category No. 1—Flowers
1-800-356-9377 (1-800-FLOWERS)
This is just like having your own personal florist 24/7.
Possibilities are virtually limitless. Immediate next-day
delivery is available almost anywhere.
What are you waiting for?

Category No. 2—Chocolate
Godiva Direct 1-800-946-3482
Lila's Chocolates (long-stem chocolate roses)
1-415-383-8887
The importance of this category cannot be overlooked.
If you're wondering whether the supposed aphrodisiac
qualities attributed to chocolate are true, they are.
Still unconvinced? Do yourself a favor. Read *Chocolate:
The Consuming Passion* by Sandra Boynton.

Category No. 3—J. Peterman
1-800-231-7341
The most unique catalog this side of heaven.
Vintage-inspired men's and women's apparel, exceptional
gifts, and distinctive stuff from faraway places.

Category No. 4—Victoria's Secret
1-800-888-8200
Great intimate gifts, including
fantastic end-of-season sales.

"How much better than wine is your love,

and the scent of your perfumes than all spices."

SONG OF SOLOMON 4:10

Ideas for Romancing Your Wife

- Put her photo on a T-shirt and wear it.
- Make her the biggest banana split she has ever eaten.
- Draw a picture of her.
- Use chopsticks to feed each other.
- Tell her you love her.
- Arrange to have flowers delivered while having dinner with her.
- Scratch her back.
- Polish the silverware.
- Scrub the pots and pans.
- Change her automobile oil.
- Make a donation in her name.
- Name a star after her.
- Have an artist paint her portrait and frame it.

- Give her monogrammed handkerchiefs.
- Bake a pie for her.
- Support a child in her name.
- Subscribe for her to her favorite magazine.
- Take a walk.
- Wash her car.
- Weed her garden.
- Cultivate her garden.
- Iron her blouses.
- Photograph her.
- Send her a tape of you singing "Happy Birthday."
- Go on a nature walk; do bird watching.
- Take a bus tour of your city.
- Take her horseback riding.
- Write a poem about her.

- Adopt a path through the woods, a sidewalk, or street.
- Visit a toy store and play with the toys.
- Test-drive cars at a dealership.
- Pretend you have unlimited amounts of money to spend and go to the shopping center.
- Do a winter picnic.
- Have your photo taken together.
- Fix a meal for the both of you and eat without utensils.
- Do the fondue thing with cheese, meat, and fruit.
- Find the best elevator ride in your town.
- Take her to a hill to watch the sun rise.
- Purchase a disposable camera and photograph her. Be sure to ask for doubles at the one-hour development lab.
- Do your "Stupid Human Trick(s)" for her.
- Tickle her.
- Select a special perfume or scent for her.
- Rent a hot tub for her.
- Take her to an art museum.
- Sponsor her to take a course like Outward Bound or CPR.
- Hire one of her friends to be her chauffeur for a day.
- Be the motor that swings the hammock.
- Plan a picnic for her at the park, arboretum, under a bridge, parking lot, lake, backyard, football field, etc.
- Give her a pedicure/manicure.
- Send her on a secret weekend travel excursion. Hand her the tickets and information just before she leaves.
- Take her on a carriage or sleigh ride.
- Drive to a darkened area late at night. Lay on top of the car and watch the sky show.
- Draw or create a dream map for her life.
- Grant a wish of hers.

No one

could ever take

your place

THANK YOU ARE AN